DOG Parties

How to Party with Your Pup

DOG Parties

How to Party with Your Pup

By Arden Moore
Illustrations by Buck Jones

BOWTIE
PRESS

Irvine, California

Karla Austin, Business Operations Manager
Jen Dorsey, Associate Editor
Michelle Martinez, Editor
Rebekah Bryant, Editorial Assistant
Ruth Strother, Editor-at-Large
Nick Clemente, Special Consultant
Vicky Vaughn, Book Designer

The recipes on pages 68 and 69 are reprinted with permission. They first appeared as Bow-Wow Brownies and Bow-Wow Brownie Frosting in *Real Food for Dogs* by Arden Moore. © 2001 Storey Books.

The dogs in this book are referred to as *he* and *she* in alternating chapters.

Library of Congress Cataloging-in-Publication Data

Moore, Arden.
  Dog parties: how to party with your pup / by Arden Moore; illustrations by Buck Jones.
     p. cm.
  ISBN 1-931993-26-2 (soft cover : alk. paper)
  1. Parties for dogs. I. Jones, Buck, ill. II. Title.

  SF427.45.M66 2004
  636.7'083—dc22

                                        2004003345

BowTie® Press
A Division of BowTie Inc.
3 Burroughs
Irvine, California 92618

Printed and Bound in Singapore
10 9 8 7 6 5 4 3 2 1

Dedication

For Chipper, my party-loving canine pal; my friends, Elise Curry, Flo and Frank Frum, and Jim Flynn; and my siblings, Deb, Karen, and Kevin. I would also like to give a special thanks to dog trainer Susan Greenbaum for all her creative tips.

—Arden

I would like to thank the dogs who have enriched my life from my childhood to present day with their love and companionship—Chico, a rat terrier; Ladybug, a Shetland sheepdog; Samantha, a dalmatian; and Blaze, a basset hound. Each was special and different. They were and are family.

—Buck

Contents

Introduction   9

Why Celebrate?   13

Location, Location, Location   21

Who to Invite and Invitation-Making Tips   37

Create a Doggone Cool Party Scene   47

Food Fit for a Dog—and You!   61

Gr-r-reat Games   71

Map Out Your Party Plans   87

Introduction

I have a confession to make. During my life, I've hosted and attended parties celebrating weddings, high school graduations, 30th birthdays, babies, Halloween, and new homes. Sure, the food treated my taste buds; the decorations adorned the place in inviting colors; and the conversations (for the most part) proved engaging. But nothing compares to hosting a dog party.

When Jazz, my corgi, graduated from puppy and basic obedience school, I rushed to make plans to celebrate his accomplishment in style: a backyard dog party. I quickly e-mailed the invites to a half-dozen friends and their doggy pals. And guess what? The RSVPs came back faster than for any other party I've hosted and EVERYONE who was invited showed up—on time and wearing grins in anticipation.

My backyard turned into a canine wonderland without a lot of expense. There's no need to invest a lot of time and money in creating fancy decorations. My back porch turned into a relay race site. Pieces of hot dogs bobbed in ankle-high water inside a light blue plastic kiddie pool. Canine tunes blared from the stereo speakers—woof! I served plenty of dog and people treats and handed out parting gifts.

The two hours sped by, filled with hearty laughs and playful yelps. Everyone genuinely enjoyed themselves. Why should anyone be surprised? When it comes to party trends, dog parties win paws down. Every year, more than ten million people celebrate their dogs' birthdays and two million bake a cake. Another million host canine parties for other reasons. These numbers are growing faster than a Labrador retriever puppy! The reason is simple: more and more people want to celebrate the events of their dog's lives just as much as they do for their children, spouses, partners, and close friends.

Snicker if you will, but deep down inside, you know that you'd much rather attend a dog party than a snobby wine-tasting affair, a pricey candle party, or a put-you-to-sleep Monopoly marathon. Admit it—wouldn't you like to receive an invite to a dog party? Or, even better, host one? People parties are passé—dog parties rule!

Everything you need to know to host—and attend—a pawsitively gr-r-reat dog party is contained in this book. Paw through these pages and get ready to have a howling good time!

Paws Up!
Arden Moore

Why Celebrate?

Think like your dog for a moment. What gets her excited? A tasty treat? A game of fetch? Playing with the neighbor's boxer? Perhaps all of the above? Dog parties offer all of these and more.

Dogs are born party animals. They like to romp. They like to chase. They like to play wrestle. They like to be included in activities, which explains why sometimes your dog puts the leash in her mouth and trots after you as you attempt to head out the garage door to go to work. They like to meet and greet, which explains why your dog pulls on the leash during a walk in the park the second she spots another friendly, leash-walked canine approaching.

Dog parties provide you with a wonderful opportunity to harness the power of play. This is your golden chance to initiate play with a purpose. You can sneak in reinforcement of doggy manners ("Good sit!"), practice basic obedience commands like wait, and

try cool tricks like Give Me a High 10! with your dog tingling with the excitement of the party. She will want to comply with your instructions because of the canine payoffs: a place to show off in front of a crowd; an opportunity to play games and socialize with dogs of all shapes, sizes, and ages; and, most importantly, a chance to consume oodles of great-tasting treats. She'll soon catch on that the better behaved she is, the better the rewards. Parties promote dog training in an enjoyable atmosphere. Dogs learn when they are having fun. Dog parties also harbor other perks. Your dog gets a chance for an aerobic workout.

If you engage the canine party attendees in a game of fetch the ball, within 10 minutes they'll return, tongues hanging out and grinning from ear to ear. The best part is that when you return home later that day, your dog will be relaxed and will want to snooze. Remember, a tired dog is a happy dog.

PLEASE, YOU FIRST.

Reasons to Party

Here are some great reasons to throw a party, but you don't really need a reason:

- Adoption anniversary
- Agility ribbon winner
- Bark mitzvahs
- Basic obedience graduation
- Birthdays
- Canine weddings
- Christmas
- Dog's 10th birthday
- Feast of St. Francis of Assisi pet blessing
- Fundraiser for local animal shelter
- Halloween
- Hanukkah
- Meet dogs in the local park
- Puppy school graduation
- Puppy's 1st birthday
- St. Patrick's Day
- Thanksgiving
- Valentine's Day
- Why-not party

Dog parties are also perfect places to hone socialization skills. A timid dog may learn to overcome her shyness when motivated by a game that offers a food reward. A young dog can watch and learn good behavior displayed by some "senior" party guests. A slightly pushy dog can learn to wait her turn to play a game or get a piece of cake.

Dogs aren't the only ones who benefit. You do, too. Think back to the last party you attended. Did you *really* enjoy yourself? Or did you purposely park your car to allow for a quick getaway? Did you fiddle with finger foods while desperately trying to come up with something witty to say? Did you get trapped by the party's egomaniac who bombarded you with brag after brag about himself? Did you worry about whether you dressed right or whether your hair looked good? Did you find yourself daydreaming about being somewhere else?

Dog parties let people relax, laugh, and not take themselves too seriously. You don't have time to fret about whether or not your outfit is going to draw compliments. Odds are that within the first half hour, your dog—or another dog—will playfully bound your way, greet you, and deposit dirty paw prints or drool droplets on your clothing.

You don't need to worry about making a witty comment, either. At these parties, dogs take center stage, not people. All eyes—and ears—are on watching a beagle nose out a Rottweiler in a best-trick contest, or on an over-excited Lab puppy getting her person tangled in her long leash. You find yourself enjoying the present moment, not lamenting about last week's work demands or next week's dental appointment.

Dog parties bolster the connection between people and canines. By bringing your dog to a canine fete, you up your "stock value" in your dog's eyes. She views you as the person who brings her to cool outings. She sees you laugh and wants to share in that joy. Parties deliver a break from the ho-hum routine you may have with your dog. Instead of that typical Saturday half-hour walk you make on the same path every week, the two of you can attend a party with plenty of new sights, sounds, and smells. A true doggy delight! Plus since the two of you must work as a team to capture the top prizes in some games, dog parties are also a fun place to work on your people-dog communication skills.

Whether simple or elaborate, indoors or outside, dog parties guarantee that all guests leave grinning.

Host a Puppy Shower

You don't even need a dog to host a party. Susan Greenbaum, a creative dog trainer who operates Barking Hills Country Club in Milford, New Jersey, suggests you host a puppy shower a month or so *before* your new four-legged friend arrives. Or, make this suggestion to a soon-to-be dog owner and offer to co-host the party.

Puppy showers generally follow the same rules as bridal or baby showers. Invite some of your dog-experienced friends who have raised pups. Consider registering your puppy shower at a local pet supply store. That way, your guests can bring toys and other puppy essentials to help you on your way. In the world of fast-growing puppies, you can never have enough chew toys, especially if your new arrival is a Labrador retriever, who lives by the motto Chew Until Two.

Treat your friends to fun and good food. Call up your bakery and request a bone-shaped cake to add to the party's theme. Or create a bone-shaped pizza. Stick with a canine theme for your decorations, too.

Test your guests' dog trivia knowledge by playing Canine Charades. Before the party, jot down the titles of dog movies, books, songs, and famous canine stars on index cards. Then divide your guests into teams and have them act out the titles for their teammates. Some ideas: *Best in Show*, *101 Dalmatians*, "(How Much Is) That Doggie in the Window" and "Hound Dog."

As part of the puppy shower, encourage guests to share some of their puppy survival tips to help you better prepare for your new tail-wagging pal. Provide each guest with a special dog treat to give to his or her canine pal at home.

Location, Location, Location

You may be blessed with a personality-plus dog, know oodles of fun games to play, and be ready to serve doggone great treats, but don't discount the importance of *where* you host your dog party. The locale can be pivotal in ensuring your party earns paws-up praise.

Before you start announcing your party or mailing out invitations, invest the time to size up your party locale options. Factor in your budget, time availability, and number of guests. You can stage the affair in your living room, backyard, or basement, or at a local park, dog-training center, upscale boarding facility, or doggy bakery. You have many choices, but recognize that no place is perfect. You need to weigh the advantages and drawbacks of each before making your selection.

To help you decide, here are some guidelines to consider:

- How much money do you plan to spend on the party? You can easily host a party in your home or backyard for less than $50. Expect to pay $100 or more if you wish to reserve use of a park, dog center, or other dog-friendly place.

- How many guests do you wish to invite? Cozy affairs with less than six dogs can be accommodated at your home. Big parties with ten or more dogs require added supervision, so a dog-training center or boarding facility might be more appropriate.

- How soon do you want to host the party? Places outside the home may require booking at least a month in advance.

Party at Home

If you choose your home—or backyard—you don't have to worry about spending money to rent a place or worry about whether the place is going to be available on the date you desire. As a general rule, limit the invitation list to no more than five dogs if you are hosting the party in your living room, and eight to ten dogs for a backyard area of 40- by 50-feet. Survey your yard and home and run through this checklist:

- Is your backyard fenced in to keep all guests, including likely-to-roam mutts, from jumping over and escaping?
- Is the entrance gate stable and easily closed?

❧ Have you dog-proofed your backyard by removing dangerous items, such as rakes and weed-killing products, filling in any holes, and patching up any openings in the fence?

❧ Did you clean your yard, getting rid of any standing water (a breeding ground for mosquitoes), weeds, and broken down furniture?

❧ Is your yard big enough to accommodate rambunctious canines with separate areas for games, food, and a canine bathroom space?

Party Profile

Abigail's Park Bash

Each spring, Debra Graham, of Washington, D.C., heralds the birthday of Abigail, her nearly three-year-old tri-colored beagle. And, yes, she does mail out party invitations in advance. Her favorite party place is a nearby park that attracts lots of dog-walking people.

"For Abigail's first birthday party, thirty people and their dogs showed up and last year, fifty people and their dogs attended," says Graham, a technical writer. She happily provided coffee, orange juice, hot chocolate, and dough-nuts for the people. On the eve of each party she stayed up all night with a friend making a table full of homemade dog treats for Abigail and her canine guests to enjoy throughout the party.

At each birthday party, the dogs romped and played, taking time out only to devour the homemade treats and lap up water. Other than a dog urinating on the agility tunnel and another dog being sent home for picking fights with the other dogs, the parties were a howling success.

"I probably spent about $200 on each party, but it is well worth it," says Graham. "Since I got Abigail as a puppy and started walking her, I've met a lot of great people. I used to be a workaholic, but now, thanks to Abigail, I have a lot of great friends."

And what are the plans for Abigail's third birthday bash?

"I'm thinking about hiring a dog massage therapist who can set up a booth and give dogs one-minute massages for a dollar," says Graham. "It could be the social event of the year."

- Will the sound of howling, yapping dogs annoy your neighbors? Consider checking with them in advance.
- Do you have adequate parking in your driveway or street to cater to all your guests?
- Do you have access to tents in case it starts to rain? Can you move the party inside?
- If you host the party indoors, can dogs go outside easily to use the bathroom? Are cleanup bags readily available?
- Do you have a room in the house big enough for all guests so dogs are not too close to one another—especially during food serving and when the honored dog "opens" his presents?
- Have you removed any breakables, such as knickknacks on tabletops, or dog hazards, such as bowls of chocolate or poisonous plants, from the room?
- Can you adequately block off other rooms to prevent dogs from roaming into off-limit places, such as your bedroom or bathrooms? Close doors or use doggy gates.
- Do you have enough chairs and couches for all the people invited?
- Can you handle dog drool, muddy paws, and spilled drink and food in your home?

Dog-Welcoming Parks

If you opt to host your party at a local park that permits dogs, be sure to contact the local government officials in advance. You may need to obtain a permit, show proof that each dog is current on

his vaccinations, or heed certain rules about where in the park you can host the party. Find out if the park allows dogs to be off leash. If not, make sure your guests know this rule. Always scope out the park's layout in advance to make sure it is suitable for your party needs.

Humane shelters are expanding their identities. No longer simply places to adopt pets, train dogs, or board dogs or cats, some shelters are also venturing into the party hosting business. Depending on the location, activities involved, food served, and number of dogs invited, shelter-hosted parties can range from $50 to $200 for two hours of fun.

Sample Party Waiver

Some animal shelters, dog-training centers, and boarding facilities may require party hosts and guests to adhere to certain rules to ensure safety for all. Expect to agree in writing in advance to their rules. Here is a sample of a party waiver from the Humane Society of the Willamette Valley in Salem, Oregon:

To ensure the safety of all participants, please read and initial the following:

___ I assure my companion animal(s) in attendance is current on all vaccinations and is appropriately licensed (where required by law).

___ I also agree to obey all laws (including picking up after my dog), exercise safety precautions, avoid littering, and respect the property of others.

___ I understand that the off-leash area is surrounded by a fence only 4-feet high. It is my duty to ensure my dog stays within this area.

___ I will remain with my dog(s) at all times and understand we will be asked to leave if my dog shows aggression toward other dogs or people.

I have read and understood the above statements. I hereby waive and release any and all rights and claims for damages I have against the Humane Society of Willamette Valley, the organizers of this party, their associates and representatives.

Signature_____

Printed name_____

Dog-Welcoming Centers

With dog parties growing in popularity, finding a place to cater to your canine's needs is getting easier. The plus of having your party away from your house is that you don't have to fuss with cleanup. In addition, these places commonly offer a lot of doggy amenities such as dog trainers, party food, and party decorations. The drawback is that using one of these venues costs more than home parties.

Places like Barking Hounds Village Lofts in Atlanta cater to owners looking for safe, supervised indoor sites to celebrate memorable occasions for their beloved dogs. They offer four centers in the Atlanta area for parties of any occasion.

"It's definitely a growing business because it is acceptable now to be crazy about your dog and we treat a dog's birthday like one would for a child," says Kim Zimmerman, marketing manager. "It is a very special day that deserves to be celebrated in style."

Prices are based on the number of dogs invited, the time reserved, and the type of food and activities desired, says Zimmerman. A 90-minute party for six dogs, for example, costs about $100 but comes with a perk: attendants quickly scoop up doggy deposits.

Barking Hounds sends out formal invitations with the honored dog's name in calligraphy. Guests receive party hats and the "top dog" wears a crown. Dogs can enjoy all-natural dog biscuits dipped in yogurt or peanut butter.

In New York City, a popular canine place to party is Biscuits & Bath Doggy Village, offering five floors of fun, including an indoor

canine track and a 30-foot long, 4-feet deep pool. John Ziegler, who co-owns the place with his mother, Sandy, has hosted birthdays, Sunday brunches, bark mitzvahs, and the occasional puppy-love wedding. The first doggy wedding involved an exchanging of "vows" between Cinder and Max Horn, a pair of mixed-breed shepherds. Cinder wore a veil and Max sported a bow tie and white collar. Each dog vowed to take the paw of the other in sickness and in health and to "faithfully promise never to bark at or bite each other except in loving play."

"The wonderful thing about these doggy parties is that they give friends a chance to gather and include other members of

Party Profile

Riley Prefers a Catered Affair

In Atlanta, Carol Sellers, a local realtor, was looking for some way to celebrate the third birthday of Riley, her golden retriever. After doing some research and con-

sulting her dog-loving friends, Sellers opted to host the bash at the Barking Hounds Village Lofts.

"I discovered that I fretted more about this party than any child's party I've given," says Sellers. "I didn't want to

have the party at my house and worry if any guest would make a mess and I didn't want to worry about weather being a factor. This place was ideal because there were enough dog trainers around that if any dog snapped or got out of line, they could step in and give them a time out and maintain control."

About a dozen dog guests attended. One small terrier spent most of the time in a chair for trying to nip, but the biggest guest, a Rottweiler, earned praise for his friendly-to-all behavior. The party's highlight was an obstacle course that an agility trainer set up. The course allowed each dog the opportunity to plunge through plastic tunnels, sail over hurdles, and gingerly walk across a dog walk. Riley showed her guests the right way to master clearing hurdles. "The party lasted about two hours and by the time Riley got home, she was down for the count and just slept the rest of the day," says Sellers.

their families, their canine pals," says Ziegler. "Here, we view people not as dog owners, but as canine parents. I can't think of a better way to honor our pets than with a great party."

Members of Biscuits & Bath receive price discounts for dog parties that can range in price from a simple affair for a $150 to renting an entire floor and inviting up to fifty guests at a price tag of $3000.

In Los Angeles, one of the "in" dog-party places is Hollywood Hounds, which Maya Prestin operates. The facility features a fenced-in backyard with a gazebo, perfect for doggy weddings or birthday bashes. For about $250, you can host a two-hour birthday party that includes decorations, cakes for people and for dogs, sodas, water, games, party hats, music, and complimentary photos for all guests. If money is not an issue, you can spend up to $1,700 for a dog wedding. The wedding package includes party trays, picking up and dropping off guests, musicians, red carpet, real flower decorations, grooming for the bride and groom, cake for people, cake for dogs, mineral water, and champagne. The "groom" wears a doggy-sized tuxedo and the "bride" wears a wedding dress and veil.

"Dog weddings are very popular," says Prestin. "Dogs that are very bonded to one another 'get married' for the fun of it."

Who to Invite and Invitation-Making Tips

A key to your party's success depends on who you invite. You need to know how to select true "party animals" from the rest of the pack and screen out dogs who may be destructive or unruly and spoil the party. This is where you need to hold your ground and not act against your better instincts. If you know your best friend's dog has initiated fights with other dogs, invite your friend—but not her dog. Explain why. This is for the safety of all guests, including her dog. You can always make sure she receives a party favor bag of goodies to bring home to her dog.

You can hedge off many problems if you simply do not invite dogs who you don't know and who are pushy or aggressive with other dogs. Not sure if a dog you want to invite is comfortable around other dogs? Before you plan your invite list, offer to go to a

local dog park with your dog, your friend, and her dog. Watch how her dog behaves around other dogs at the dog park. Dogs who are regular attendees at local dog parks seem to display the best temperaments at parties because they are used to being around all kinds of canines.

Depending on your party, you may want to exercise caution about inviting intact males, especially if your attendees include young, neutered males. You may be setting up a situation for a battle of male dominance. Same goes for senior dogs with health issues. If the majority of the guests are energetic young dogs, the senior dog may become grouchy and not want to interact with them. You can always invite the senior dog, but let her safely watch the festivities on the sidelines.

What about dogs who are downright friendly—until it comes to filled food bowls and they turn into resource guarders? One solution is to identify dogs as resource guarders or those who tend to be a bit grouchy or snappy. Have them wear red bandannas that you provide as they arrive. Give the other doggy guests blue bandannas. The red bandanna alerts the people guests to give this dog ample space when she is eating. Owners of the red bandanna dogs can also make sure their dogs are far from the others when people begin doling out cake slices or treats.

You also need to consider the energy levels of your doggy guests. Don't be fooled by size. The bigger the dog doesn't always equate to more energy. Your sister's Jack Russell terrier can probably run circles around your best friend's Great Dane.

Welcome to Yappy Hour

Happy hour is so passé. If you really want to be trendy, why not participate in yappy hour? Places like the Humane Society of Southern Arizona in Tucson are discovering that the cool party place these days is at their shelter when it hosts yappy hour.

JoAnn Spencer, animal outreach program manager, realized that her shelter had plenty of obedience and agility classes, but she was looking for a structured social

event that offered a fun release involving people and their dogs. And so yappy hour was born. People and their dogs meet at a training center near the shelter that offers 5,600 square feet inside and two large, fenced grassy outdoor areas. At a rate of $10 per person, yappy hour features a canine menu that includes turkey burgers, beef jerky, dog biscuits, and a dog version of Popsicles. Yappy hour has been such a success at this Tucson shelter that Spencer says they plan to offer them monthly and add holiday themes.

For people, yappy hour menu ideas include meat and cheese trays, fruit trays, shrimp cocktails, carrot cake, chili, and chocolate-covered strawberries. Make sure to provide plenty of water and sodas to quench thirsts.

Spencer offers a few other pointers. Position a hose within easy reach in case two canine guests decide to tangle. Announce to guests that they are responsible for picking up after their own dogs. Place plastic bag holders on a fence or other accessible place to make doggy cleanup easy.

Next Challenge: Creating the Invitations

Congratulations! You've nailed down the venue and decided who is coming. Now for the next big challenge: creating invitations that convey the right message. You can buy party invitations from your

local card store or pet supply store, or you can go online and order from dog party Web sites. If you want to save money and personalize your invitations, try creating your own. You can use a computer software program or make handmade invitations using colored construction paper, scissors, glue, stickers, rubber stamps, paint, crayons, or colored markers.

On invitations, do not assume anything. Spell out your rules and requests clearly. Unlike most people parties, where it can be fashionable to arrive late, emphasize that your party has a definite starting and stopping time. Dog parties work best when guests arrive and leave at the same time. It is also advisable to request that people do NOT bring their dog's favorite toys or treats with them. These items could spark a jealous snit among canine guests. You can, however, indicate on the invitation that you will serve refreshments at the party. If you're planning the party at an outdoor locale such as a park, request B.Y.O.P.B. (Bring Your Own Poop Bags) on the invitations. Of course, you will have extra bags on hand, but you don't want to run out!

Practice Miss Doggy Manners by mailing out the invitations a month in advance and request that guests let you know if they plan on attending or not. Confirm the guest list a few days before the party. A couple of other inside tips: Check in advance with your guests that the day you plan for the party is free for most of them. Find out if they—or their dogs—have any food allergies. Some dogs are allergic to wheat and some people are allergic to peanuts. Know the "no-no" foods and avoid them in the homemade or store-bought foods that you choose for your party.

Slip a small dog biscuit in the envelope with your invitation to entice the canine guests. If you do not wish to receive any gifts for your dog's birthday party, you could help animals in need. Ask your guests for donations to your local humane society. Request

that the gifts be made in your dog's name. As a courtesy to your guests, provide donation forms and stamped envelopes addressed to the humane society.

What to Include on the Invitations

Whether you decide to buy party invitations, make them on the computer, or create them by hand, all the invitations must include the following information:

- Your name
- Your dog's name
- The occasion or reason for the party
- Date and time of the party
- Hours of the party—aim for two hours max
- Party location, address, and directions
- Phone number and e-mail address for RSVPs
- Party rules (request that all canine guests be kept on leashes until they are instructed otherwise)
- Indicate whether refreshments will be served
- If you're hosting an outdoor party, it's a good idea to include a rain date.
- If the occasion is a birthday party and you do not want presents, ask for a donation to the local humane society.

Create a Doggone Cool Party Scene

Your invitations are in the mail. Guests are excitedly responding with "Yes! We Will Attend!" In the weeks or days leading up to your party, you need to map out decorations, music, a menu, and activities. You also need to determine the party flow.

When it comes to decorations, keep it simple. Avoid balloons. A burst balloon can spook a dog, and balloon material can cause choking if a canine guest swallows it. Skip flower arrangements, too. Most dogs could care less about petunias, and some flowers and plants are poisonous to dogs. Instead, invest the money in tennis balls to give to each dog as parting gifts. If you plan on using streamers or banners, hang them high enough to be out of paw's reach.

Create Party Zones

Map out areas for food serving, activities, and doggy bathrooms. For outdoor parties, consider using colored squeeze chalk (available at hardware stores). It washes off easily with water. Outline the poop zone in the far corner of the party—as far away from the food zone as possible. You can also use the chalk to indicate start and finish lines for games.

Create colorful signs for each party zone. Unleash your imagination. For example, cut out yellow construction paper in the shape of a fire hydrant to identify the poop zone. Make sure that this zone has plenty of disposable bags, a scooper, and a big garbage can with a plastic liner and a secure lid. Cut out a giant blue dog bone for the food serving area and a Frisbee-shaped red sign to identify the activities zone. Keep all food—for people and

their dogs—safely out of paw's reach until it is time to serve. For home parties, you can keep the food on the kitchen counters but pushed back to stop large dogs from any counter-surfing activities.

Select canine tunes to play from a portable stereo to add to the party's ambience. Favorite songs include: "Hound Dog," "Snoopy and the Red Baron," "Who Let the Dogs Out?," and the theme from *Scooby Doo.*

Provide some extra leashes and collars in case some guests arrive with dogs off leash. Give friendly reminders as the guests arrive to keep dogs on leashes until you indicate leash-off time.

Make party hats optional. Some dogs love them; others loathe them.

Provide Arrival Activities

An arrival activity is a must. You can create a giant birthday card out of poster board. Use safe finger paint. Have each guest put their paw prints on the card with their human signing their name. Keep a bucket and towels nearby to wash off the paws after they leave their autographs for the honored dog.

You can also welcome guests and guide them to a table set up with Kongs in a variety of sizes. Identify the name of each canine guest on an appropriately sized Kong. At this table, provide an array of foods to stuff inside the Kongs: peanut butter, Cheese Whiz, small dog biscuits, liver treats, chopped raw carrots, and other doggy delights. Store these finished Kongs out of paw's reach and bring them out when the honored dog opens his

presents. The doggy guests will be distracted by their Kongs and ignore the honored dog pawing through his gifts.

To keep the party moving, always aim to play two or three games or contests before serving the birthday cake. This gives canine guests the opportunity to unleash some energy. Save opening presents until the end.

In Chapter 6, you will find an assortment of indoor and outdoor games to consider playing. If you are looking for quick contests, consider any of these:

🐾 Be a Clothes Hound. Set up a pile of old shirts, socks, scarves, hats, and shorts in a corner. The goal: How many clothes can you get on your dog in 60 seconds? You determine the winner.

🐾 The Sloppiest Kisser. Ask for a brave volunteer to be smooched by each canine guest. Select the dog who delivers the wettest kiss.

🐾 Best Popcorn Catcher. If your party sports a lot of canine jocks, have each person toss pieces of air-popped popcorn to their dog pals. The winner: The dog who catches the most popcorn pieces in a row or snags the popcorn from the farthest distance.

Help canine guests release some pent-up energy at the start of the party by having them perform doggy push-ups. This is a quick

Party Profile

Sami Parties Indoors

In San Diego, Janet Wytrych opted for a small, indoor evening gathering to celebrate birthday number one for Sami, her golden retriever. The guest list included Bronski, a yellow Labrador; Kaleo, a yellow Labrador;

and Sheena, a Newfoundland. Plus, of course, their people pals.

She held the party in her home's kitchen and family room areas. She began with each doggy guest receiving a party hat, nosing one another, and playfully chasing one another. Then Wytrych called Sami over to a table full of gifts.

"Sami had never opened presents before, but by the end of the night, he had this gift-opening concept down," laughs Wytrych, a systems analyst. "Now, whenever Sami hears the sound of gift wrapping, he gets very excited and rushes over."

The party ended with each canine partyer diving into slices of peanut butter flavored cake from a doggy bakery while their owners sang "Happy Birthday" to a smiling Sami. As a thank you, Wytrych provided each guest with treat-filled bags for party favors.

series of *sit* and *down* commands done so it looks like your dog is doing push-ups—canine style. Or, line up all the dogs and have them perform synchronized commands like *sit, roll over,* and *shake a paw.* Be sure to reward participants with treats.

Anticipate dog snits and be prepared in advance. Establish a doggy time out area marked off with baby gates or other barriers to separate a grouchy dog from the rest of the guests to give him time to cool off. Keep garden hoses or buckets of water nearby or have cans with pennies and lids to make loud noises. The water and the noise can distract sparring dogs. Never use your hands to separate feuding dogs because you risk being bitten. To reinforce good doggy manners in a fun way, consider hiring a dog trainer or agility instructor to provide some canine entertainment. You can call your local dog-training club to request an instructor to come and teach some fun tricks to your guests.

Dog trainer Susan Greenbaum, of Barking Hills Country Club in Milford, New Jersey, says a game growing in popularity at her dog parties is based on a new dog sport called rally. She suggests you hire a rally instructor for your party. This new sport involves a series of instructional signs. Each dog and his person go to a sign and if the sign says, "stop, sit," the dog must perform those commands. Then go to the next sign, which might read, "right turn and then sit down." The next sign might read, "take one step forward, halt, and then take two steps forward, halt."

You can rent or buy agility equipment for dogs to race through and climb on. Or, if you are handy and know your way

around a hardware store, opt for an inexpensive alternative. You can create agility-like hurdles using PVC piping (or just prop a long-handled broomstick on top of two chairs). Make tunnels from giant cardboard boxes (such as moving boxes used to hold clothing or appliance boxes). For parties with small dogs, you can also drape a bed sheet over a card table to serve as a makeshift tunnel.

Throughout the party, cheerfully announce leash-on and leash-off times. Definitely keep leashes on whenever serving food. Save time at the end of the party for gift opening. Immediately throw away all ribbons, bows, and wrapping paper to keep dogs from eating them. Remember to serve the customized Kongs to canine guests while the honored dog opens his gifts.

Party Profile

Halloween Party for BB and Bullet

In Columbia, Missouri, Lindsee Billings took advantage of her home's location and large, fenced backyard to host a Halloween party with her pair of beagles, BB and Bullet. She lives close to the interstate in an area where

barking partygoers wouldn't disturb her neighbors. Her house is free of carpet and features a fenced yard that even the tallest of canines could not escape.

The Halloween party was a success because of pre-planning and cooperation from her guests. She shares a few lessons to others planning parties:

* Pick up any dog toys in the yard and house before the party to help prevent canine fights.

* Create a puppy-only area to separate the young pups from the bigger, older dogs.

* Know the personalities of all dogs invited to avoid aggressive guests.

* Instruct each human guest that they need to be responsible for their individual dogs to avoid any food or resource guarding issues.

No party is complete without prizes for winning games and parting gifts. The goal is to make sure no canine guest leaves without some prize or party memento. To make your party extra special, offer one-minute massages, trick training lessons, or photo sessions using a digital camera. You can e-mail the images to your guests within a day or two after the party.

Here are some prize possibilities:

- a $10 gift certificate to a local doggy bakery
- collapsible water bowl for people to use when they take their dogs on car trips, hikes, and other activities
- designer collar with a gift certificate to have the winning dog's name embroidered
- doggy picture frame
- non-skid food or water bowl
- year subscription to *Dog Fancy* magazine

Here are some items to consider when creating your party favors:

- a $5 gift certificates to a pet supply store
- canine first-aid kits containing items like tweezers, veterinary wrap, and ice packs
- colored tennis balls or Frisbees
- poop bags that clip on a leash
- treat bags filled with dog biscuits and marked with each dog's name
- window stickers to alert the fire department that a house contains pets

Food Fit for a Dog—and You!

sk any dog and she will readily tell you—if she could—that food rules her life and her thoughts. You can bring out the real chowhounds in your party by serving some homemade treats or store-bought goodies. Pamper your guests by serving bottled or filtered water in their drinking bowls. As a party favor, provide stylish ceramic water bowls and personalize them with each guest's name.

If you are not up for being a canine chef, rely on the experts. Select your party's treats from a local doggy bakery or order online selections in advance from a dog bakery Web site. Don't go hog-wild on portions or on the amount of food. You don't want your guests to get aching tummies from eating too much, too rapidly. Equally important is to use labels to identify which foods are for people and which foods are for dogs. Some doggy treats can look very much like people snacks.

When it comes to chow, some dogs can be downright ugly to any—and all—dogs who come near their party food. When you're ready to dole out the slices of canine cake or other doggy dishes, instruct all the people to put their dogs on leashes. Give each of them a hula hoop. Space the hula hoops on the ground so that none touch. Then ask guests and their dogs to stay inside their own hula hoops while the dogs woof down the food. Reuse the hula hoops later in the party by having agile canines leap through them.

Never allow dogs to share food from the same bowl or plate. Always space the dogs apart. Your dog may be mellow at your home and around dogs she knows, but she can turn into a protective bully when it comes to eating her piece of birthday cake at a party with some dogs she does not know. Provide plenty of water bowls. Monitor the water bowls frequently, especially if you are hosting an outdoor party in hot weather, to make sure dogs stay hydrated.

The following are some bark-a-licious recipes sure to make your party a success.

Catering Cues

If you opt to have your dog party catered, be sure to get answers in advance to these key food questions:

- What are all the ingredients in a dog birthday cake? (Make sure chocolate is not included.)
- Which party foods will need to be kept refrigerated until serving?
- Are all-natural foods used or do some dishes contain potentially harmful food additives or preservatives?
- Whenever possible, can organic ingredients be used (foods certified to be free of any harmful pesticides)?
- What is the number of servings for each prepared dish?
- Which dog biscuits or other dry treats are recommend to put in a take-home treat bag as the guests depart?

Dem Bones Biscuits

Lifetime dog lover and full-time chef Kookie Brock, of Newport Beach, California, shares this creation sure to get your canine guests drooling with delight.

Ingredients:

1/2 cup cornmeal	3 tablespoons liver powder
1/2 cup oatmeal	1/2 cup meat drippings or margarine
1 1/2 cups whole wheat flour	1 egg
1/4 cup Rye Crisp crackers, crumbled	1/2 cup beef broth
1 teaspoon garlic powder	

Preheat oven to 350 degrees Fahrenheit. Combine cornmeal, oatmeal, flour, rye crackers, garlic powder, and liver powder in a large mixing bowl. Add meat drippings (or margarine) and blend together. Mix in egg and beef broth until the batter forms a ball. Knead the mixture for a couple minutes. Roll out on a board sprinkled with flour. Use cookie cutters (in dog-themed shapes) to cut out dough. Place cutout pieces on a baking sheet sprayed with a nonstick cooking spray. Bake for 30 minutes. Remove and allow to cool before serving. This recipe makes about 40 medium-sized biscuits.

Party Pup-sicles

If your party is during the dog days of summer, curb the heat with these chill-filled treats!

Ingredients:

1 quart orange juice

1 banana, mashed

$1/2$ cup plain yogurt

Mix all ingredients together in a pitcher with a spout. Carefully pour the blend into empty ice cube trays. Store the trays in the freezer until the blend becomes solid. When ready to serve, pop the pup-sicles out of the trays into a big serving dish and hand one to each party guest.

Marvelous Mutt Meatballs

Have some fun and hone your canine guests' fetching skills by tossing a few of these meaty treats.

Ingredients:

1 pound ground beef	1 cup bread crumbs
$2/3$ cup grated cheddar cheese	2 eggs, whisked
2 carrots, finely chopped	2 tablespoons tomato paste

Preheat over to 350° F. Combine all ingredients in a large bowl. Scoop out spoonfuls of the mixture and roll into mini meatballs, each about the size of a quarter. Place the meatballs on a cookie sheet sprayed with nonstick cooking spray. Bake for 15 to 20 minutes. Cool before serving. This recipe serves 10 to 15 canine guests.

Leap for Liver

In Dyer, Indiana, canine duo Misty and Oliver start yipping and prancing whenever their owner, Karen Cichocki, brings out the liver from the refrigerator and the food processor from the cabinet. It can only mean one delicious thing: liver treats are on their way! Misty and Oliver give their paw-print seal of approval for this party treat recipe.

Ingredients:

1 pound sliced beef liver (save the juice)

$^1/_4$ cup water

1 small box corn muffin mix

Preheat the oven to 350° F. In a food processor, blend the liver one slice at a time on high until liquefied. Add a little water as you add each slice. Pour the corn muffin mix into a large bowl. Then add the liquefied liver and mix thoroughly with a large, wooden spoon. Spray an $8^1/_2$- by 11-inch baking pan with nonstick cooking spray. Pour the liver mix into the pan. Bake for 25 to 30 minutes, or until the middle springs back at the touch of your finger or wooden spoon. Cool and cut into small, bite-size cubes. Store the cubes in resealable plastic bags in the refrigerator until it is time to hand them out at the party.

Party Food Tips

Guarantee that the food you serve at your canine party is truly fit for a dog. To keep your tail-wagging guests begging for seconds, follow these nutritional guidelines for lip-smacking party success:

Serve doggy cakes made with flour, carob, vanilla, honey, and apples—all canine favorites.

Check with owners of the invited canine guests in advance to see if any dogs are on food-restricted diets or are allergic to certain foods, such as wheat. Avoid serving those foods at your party.

Say no to chocolate—even for people guests. Make sure that the canine cake and treats do not contain chocolate, which contains a potentially lethal ingredient called theobromine. Substitute any recipes calling for chocolate with carob—a sweet but safe treat.

Oust the onions. If you make any homemade recipes at your dog party, skip the onions. The sulfur in onions can cause severe anemic reactions in some dogs.

Keep perishable party foods in the refrigerator until serving.

Bowwow Brownies

Your canine party animals will howl with delight if you dish up these bark-a-licious brownies. Don't fret—these are canine-safe brownies—no chocolate. This recipe uses a safer alternative—carob.

Ingredients:

¹/₂ cup vegetable oil	1 teaspoon vanilla
2 tablespoons honey	¹/₂ cup carob chips
1 cup whole wheat flour	¹/₄ cup carob powder
4 eggs	¹/₂ teaspoon baking powder

Preheat the oven to 350° F. In a medium-sized bowl, blend the oil and honey thoroughly using a wooden spoon. Add the remaining ingredients and mix well.

Pour onto a greased 15-by10-inch baking sheet or pan. Bake for 30 to 35 minutes. Let cool, and then frost (see accompanying frosting recipe below) if desired. Cut into bite-size squares. Store any extras in a sealed container in the refrigerator as post-party treats for your dog.

Bowwow Brownie Frosting

To jazz up the party brownies, you can make this easy frosting recipe:

Ingredients:

12 ounces fat-free cream cheese	1 teaspoon honey
1 teaspoon vanilla	

In a small mixer, blend all three ingredients. Then use a spatula to spread the frosting over the can of cooled brownies.

Gr-r-reat Gravy Cookies

Your meat-loving doggy guests will *sit* on command if you serve these easy-to-make cookies. Hey, where is it written that cookies must be sweet to taste good?

Ingredients:

2$^1/_2$ cups whole wheat flour	$^1/_2$ cup nonfat dry milk
2 small jars beef-flavored baby food	$^1/_2$ cup water
6 tablespoons beef gravy	1 tablespoon brown sugar
1 egg	$^1/_2$ teaspoon salt

Preheat the oven to 350° F. Combine all ingredients in a large mixing bowl. Lightly pat your hands with flour and shape the mix into a big ball. Flatten the ball using a floured wooden rolling pin. Use a cookie cutter to cut the dough into triangles or stars—or use a dog-shaped cookie cutter for a canine-styled design. Place the cookies on a greased cookie sheet. Bake for 25 minutes, or until lightly browned. Allow the cookies to cool completely before serving.

Gr-r-reat Games

At the heart of any great dog party—besides good chow, of course—are the games. Many dog games are actually spin-off versions of popular people games like bobbing for apples, potato sack races, buried treasure hunts, and musical chairs. You are only limited by your imagination and time availability.

Successful parties offer two or three games for their guests. Some are dog only, but make sure that you include at least one game that involves people, too. After all, dogs have senses of humor. They deserve to laugh at our follies once in a while.

Use your imagination in creating games, but make sure before you start a game, everyone understands the rules. Heed this motto: The simpler, the better. Parties are meant to be exercises in fun—not confusion.

Two popular games that you can play anywhere, indoors or outdoors, are Snoopy Says and My Dog Will Eat Anything. Curious? Read on.

Snoopy Says

Who says obedience has to be boring? This is a fun way to reinforce doggy manners. This is a variation on the popular child's game Simon Says. You (as the party host) instruct all guests to line up with their dogs facing them and on leashes.

The rules are simple: the people–dog teams must comply with your command whenever you say, "Snoopy Says." For example, "Snoopy says sit your dog." People must get their dogs to sit within 5 seconds or less. But if you simply say, "Sit your dog," people should not instruct their dog to do anything.

Other commands include "Snoopy says down your dog," "Snoopy says have your dog roll over," or "Snoopy says have your dog shake paws." Teams are disqualified when they perform a command that is not preceded by the "Snoopy says" phrase or fail to perform the "Snoopy says" command. The winning team is the one that heeds all "Snoopy says" commands.

My Dog Will Eat Anything Contest

We know canines can be chowhounds. This game tests the taste bud willingness of your canine guests. A few pointers: Select dog-safe foods only. That means definitely no onions or chocolate. Start with apple slices, and work your way up to air-popped popcorn, grapes, cherry tomatoes, carrot sticks, and broccoli sprigs.

The rules are simple. Each person offers a piece of food to his or her dog who has 30 seconds in which to eat it. The teams are eliminated as dogs refuse to eat the food or spit it out. The one dog left eating is declared the chowhound champ. This game introduces healthy foods, which people can later use as low-calorie treats to keep their dogs at an ideal weight.

Dunking for Hot Dogs

Remember the fun you had as a child, bobbing for apples at Halloween parties? Or perhaps you reigned as the pie-eating champion at your local town fair. This fun outdoor game is a canine spin-off of these face-in-food games—and a perfect choice for the chowhounds on your guest list. Even dogs a bit shy about

getting their feet wet may leap into the pool floating with pieces of hot dog because they are being cheered on by their owners in a friendly atmosphere.

☙ Items needed: A plastic child's pool or a 5-gallon plastic bucket; cut-up hot dogs; a watch that can count seconds; a few towels to dry off each canine contestant.

☙ Setup: Cut one hot dog into ten bite-sized pieces. Drop them into the kiddie pool or bucket filled with about 3 inches of water.

☙ The rules: Have people keep their dogs leashed and lined up. When a dog's name is announced, instruct his owner to bring the dog to the kiddie pool and unleash him. Instruct the dog to get into the pool. As soon as he does, start the timer. The goal is for each dog to gobble up as many hot dog pieces as possible in a set time—such as 30 seconds or a full minute.

☙ The winner: The dog who eats the most pieces of hot dog in the shortest amount of time.

☙ Variation: Substitute tennis balls for pieces of hot dog. Of course with tennis balls, the object is to grab them but not eat them.

Water Relay

Who says learning has to be a chore? Some learning can be doggone fun—like heeling on a leash. This outdoor game requires people and their dogs to work as a team. It is also a fun way to reinforce a dog's need to be on a leash and walk nicely without pulling or yanking.

☙ Items needed: A bucket of water, small paper cups, six-foot leashes, and 16-ounce plastic cups. Bring out enough cups for each person–dog team.

☙ Setup: Locate the bucket with water at the starting line. Position the large plastic cups (one per person–dog team) at the finish line. Give each person a small paper cup.

☙ The rules: Each person must hold a paper cup full of water in the same hand that holds the dog's leash. All participants line up at the starting line. At the sound of a whistle, each person–dog team must stay in their lane and move quickly to their designated 16-ounce plastic cup at the finish line. When they reach the finish line, they must quickly empty the water from the paper cup into their respective plastic cup. They go back to the starting line and refill their paper cup with water from the bucket.

- ❧ The winner: The first person–dog team that fills their plastic cup with water without spilling it.
- ❧ Variation: Instead of water and paper cups, have each person try to balance a tennis ball on a large wooden spoon, using the same hand that holds their leashed dog as the pair moves toward a finish line. They must go back to the starting line if they drop the ball.

Dig and Find

Some dogs are born diggers, so here's an outdoor game that offers them an appropriate place to dig.

- ❧ Items needed: A child's hard, plastic wading pool, coarse sand, dog biscuits, and tennis balls.
- ❧ Setup: Fill the wading pool with the sand. Avoid fine sand that can irritate a dog's eyes or stick to his coat. Hide a few dog biscuits and tennis balls in the sand. Be sure to count ahead of time the number of hidden biscuits and tennis balls.
- ❧ The rules: One by one, call each dog to the sandy site. Encourage each dog to dig and to find the hidden treasures.
- ❧ The winner: The dog who finds the most buried treasures in the shortest amount of time—say, one minute.

Fetch That Ball

Test the speed and heed of your dogs with a timed tennis ball contest. This outdoor game reinforces the *come* command and showcases how well each person and dog work together as a team.

❧ Items needed: Provide one tennis ball per canine guest. Make sure each tennis ball is a different color, or use a permanent marker to number each ball, distinguishing each ball from the others. You also need a space wide and long enough to toss balls. Create a starting line as well as an end line, past which all tossed balls must cross.

❧ Setup: Line up the dogs on a starting line with each dog next to his owner. All dogs should start in the sit position. Make sure there is at least a 6- to 8-feet width between each person–dog team at the start line.

- The rules: On your *ready, set, toss!* command, have each person toss a tennis ball straight out in front and far enough that it crosses a predetermined end line. Each person must instruct his or her dog to fetch his specific ball and bring it back. Dogs who keep the ball and fail to return on the *come* command are disqualified. So are dogs who grab the wrong tennis ball. Then play a second round with the finalists.

- The winner: The dog who brings his tennis ball to his person the fastest.

Find Snow Biscuits

If you live in a snowy area and plan on inviting hardy, outdoor dogs to your party, here's an outdoor game that challenges their tracking abilities.

- Items needed: snow, dog biscuits, and a snow shovel

- Setup: Before guests arrive, dig little paths out in the snow, about 20 feet in length—one path per dog. Drop a specific number of dog biscuits into the path (remember how many!) and bury them under an inch of snow.

- The rules: Instruct each person to bring their dogs to their path starting lines and release their leashes. The goal is for each dog to sniff, find, and eat the buried biscuits.

- The winner: The dog who finds and eats the most biscuits in the shortest amount of time.

Musical Canine Chairs

So, what happens if Mother Nature decides to rain on your party plans? You need a backup plan. You can indicate on your invitation a rain-out date, or, if the guest list is small enough and you have the space, move the party indoors. Some people prefer to host indoor parties—rain or shine—inside their living rooms, basements, and rec rooms or to rent a dog-friendly place like a dog-training center.

Here's a fun indoor game to consider at your next canine gala: Musical Canine Chairs. Put to music this game reinforces your dog's need to heel and sit on command. Select tunes that are upbeat and lively.

- Items needed: Enough chairs for all participating people and a portable stereo or radio.

- Setup: As the music starts, people have their dogs heel on their left sides as they walk counterclockwise around a line of chairs that contains one fewer than the number of people.

- The rules: When the music stops, each person must sit on a chair with his or her dog (leash off) sitting on the floor to the left. People can give their dogs the sit command but cannot force them into a sitting position. Each round, remove a chair to ensure that there is always one fewer chair than there are participants.

- The winner: The person–dog team that outlasts the others with one chair left.

Let's See Some ID

Here's a chance to see how well people really know their own dogs. This indoor game works great if the majority of the dogs invited are about the same size and shape.

☙ Items needed: Dark-colored handkerchiefs or bandannas to work as blindfolds and a stopwatch.

☙ Setup: Line up dogs on one side of the room and make sure that they are all on leashes so they can't run around freely. Instruct the people guests to move to the other side of the room, far from the dogs.

☙ The rules: Blindfold each human guest, one at a time. Then bring up each similar-shaped dog to that person who must identify his or her dog. Limit each "inspection" to 5 seconds and then bring up the next dog. Make sure that any "clues" such as a uniquely designed collar or harness are not on the dog. If possible, use the same leash and collar when presenting each dog.

☙ The winner: The person who picks out his or her dog the fastest.

Test of Canine Will Power

Every dog should heed the *leave it* command. Here's an indoor game that truly tests the standing power of chowhounds.

☙ Items needed: Hot dogs and a stopwatch.

☙ Setup: Cut hot dogs in half. Make sure there are enough pieces of hot dog for each canine guest.

☙ Rules: This game reinforces the *leave it* command in a fun way. Make sure that the person–dog teams (leashes on) are far

enough apart from one another. Instruct each person to get his or her dog into a down position. Then have the contestants each place a hot dog 2 inches from their dog's nose as they say *leave it*.

🐾 The winner: The dog who resists his hot dog the longest and waits until his person pal gives him the okay to gulp it down.

Canine Obstacle Course

Got a spacious living room or basement area? You can create a mini obstacle course for canine party guests.

Items needed: Brightly colored yarn, card table, bed sheet, folding chairs, and a stopwatch.

🐾 The setup: Weave the yarn path around sturdy objects such as couches and coffee tables. Put a sheet over a card table to create a tunnel. For large dogs, have them hurdle over a folding chair. For small dogs, have them run under a folding chair.

❧ The rules: Instruct the guests on the specific route that their dogs must follow. They can give only hand signals or voice commands to guide their dogs to the right route. They cannot touch their dogs.

❧ The winner: The dog who follows his owner's directions the best and finishes the course the quickest without making any detours.

Newspaper Costume Contest

This indoor game showcases the imagination powers of your guests and the willingness of dogs to model their costume creations. This game idea is courtesy of Susan Greenbaum, a dog

Don't Forget the Prizes!

Part of the fun in winning a game is getting a prize. Here are some gr-r-reat prizes to hand out to the winning team:

- chew toys
- collar
- doggy nail pawlish
- dog picture frame
- fancy doggy water bowl or a non-skid food bowl
- food placemats
- Frisbees
- gift basket with treats
- gift certificate to a doggy bakery
- gift certificate to a local pet supply store
- herbal shampoo
- leash

trainer in Milford, New Jersey. "The less material you give your guests, the more clever people are," she declares.

☙ Items needed: A week's supply of newspapers, masking tape, and one pair of scissors per guest.

☙ The setup: Provide each guest with the same amount of newspaper sections, roll of masking tape, and pair of scissors. Position each person–dog team in a different part of the room.

☙ The rules: Each person has 10 minutes to create a costume for his or her dog using only newspaper, tape, and scissors. The dog must be willing to wear the creation.

☙ The winner: You pick the winning team that displays the most creative costume worn by the most complying dog.

Map Out Your Party Plans

When you hear the approaching bark of your first guest, you want to be ready for the festivities. That's why it is so important to make a checklist in advance—you don't want to forget anything. Plan ahead by shopping for bargains. Always give yourself at least 30 minutes of cushion time between when you THINK you will have the party ready and before the first guest appears. Some eager guests may show up early! Here is a party checklist you can use as a guide. Feel free to add more items to customize your party theme.

Party Checklist

❑ Banners and decorations (with tape or stick pins to attach)
❑ Chairs and serving tables for two-legged guests
❑ Cleanup supplies (paper towels, sponges, doggy "deposit" enzymatic cleaners)
❑ Dog cake with candles
❑ Dog treats
❑ Food plates or bowls your canine guests
❑ Game equipment
❑ Guest of honor
❑ Music and portable CD player
❑ Party hats
❑ Party prizes
❑ Party take-home favors
❑ People food, plates, and utensils
❑ Poop scoop bags, garbage bags, and trash bin

- ❏ Portable or cell phone to take calls from late-arrivals
- ❏ Spare leashes
- ❏ Water bowls
- ❏ Whistle (to grab a dog's attention to stop unwanted behavior)

Dog Party Timeline

To make sure that your party truly goes to the dogs, professional dog trainers and canine party planners say this is one party that you should not try to slap together at the last minute. Here's a working timetable for before and during the party:

Six Weeks Before

- Locate a party place if you decide to host the party outside your home. Check with local municipalities to reserve time at a dog-welcoming park. Come up with a rain date for outdoor affairs in case of inclement weather. Be prepared to put down a deposit to lock into a time at an indoor dog center.
- Decide on how much money you want to budget for the party.
- Make sure to include the cost for renting a place, food, gifts, and decorations.
- Choose a party theme. This helps in designing invitations and selecting decorations.

One Month Before

- Organize the party invitation list. Select dogs who know each other and are comfortable with other dogs. Keep the list to a

manageable number of dogs. Most dog parties average six to eight dogs.

- ☙ Mail party invitations addressed to the dog and his owner.
- ☙ Provide a map to the party location, the hours of the party, and your contact information (include your phone and e-mail address). Include a friendly reminder to owners to do poop patrol for their dogs.

One to Two Weeks Before

- ☙ Place an order for the canine cake and other doggy treats with a doggy bakery if you opt not to be a canine chef. Arrange for pickup the night before or morning of the party.
- ☙ Decide on the order of events for the party—when to serve the cake, when to play canine games, and when to open gifts.
- ☙ Shop for decorations that illustrate your party theme. Do not use balloons. The popping sound of a burst balloon can spook

a dog. If a curious dog swallowed a popped balloon, the dog could choke.

🐾 Confirm the number of attendees and check with owners to see if their dogs have any food allergies or potential behavior problems.

One Day Before

🐾 Dog-proof your home's interior by putting breakables out of paw's reach and closing off doors to bedrooms and bathrooms. Clean your enclosed yard of debris if you plan to host the party outdoors at your home. Make sure you have plenty of poop bags and trash containers with lids.

- For parties at dog-friendly parks or indoor locales, reconfirm your party's time and any guidelines with park or venue management.

Dog Party Gift Ideas

Stumped at what to give the star of the canine party? Here are some practical—and not-so-practical—ideas:

For Puppies

- a copy of *Dog Training: A Lifelong Guide* by Arden Moore
- crate
- crate bedding
- dog bone-shaped cookie cutters

It's Party Time!

On the day of the party you're going to have plenty to do. Here are some helpful hints to ensure both your human and canine guests have the best time possible.

- ❖ Provide plenty of water bowls and doggy cleanup bags.
- ❖ Keep dogs on leashes for control during introductions.
- ❖ Make party hats optional. Some dogs love them; others loathe them.

- Set up a table with dry kibble, chopped raw carrots, dog biscuits, peanut butter, and Cheese Whiz. Allow each person to stuff a Kong toy with his or her dog's favorite treat. Space out the dogs while they enjoy these treat-filled toys so that there are no food territorial issues.

- Locate food and drinks for people out of the reach of dogs.

- Play two or three games before serving the birthday cake. Let the guests unleash some energy before serving the cake and opening gifts.

- Never allow dogs to eat from the same bowl or plate. Make sure there is at least 6 feet of space between each dog while serving food.

- Limit the party to two hours.

- Provide special gift bags to hand out to each departing guests.

- Don't forget to take photos of the party. Later, send copies to the attendees.

- dog doormat
- dog note cards and envelopes
- dog towel
- gift certificate to puppy's veterinary clinic
- gift certificates to local dog groomers
- identification tag
- odor-neutralizer enzymatic cleaners such as Nature's Miracle
- puppy biscuits
- puppy potty pads
- puppy-sized chew toys
- silver rattle with puppy's name and birth date inscribed

For All Dogs

- breed-specific statuette or calendar
- canine first-aid kits
- canine seat belt
- chew toys
- collar with dog's name
- combs and brushes suitable for the dog's breed and hair coat
- dental dog chews
- dog bed
- dog blanket
- dog picture frame
- dog style food placemats
- gift certificate for a wellness checkup at the dog's veterinary clinic

- gift certificate to a local dog grooming salon
- gift certificate to a local doggy daycare center
- gift certificate to local doggy wash
- hollow, hard rubber toys to stuff with treats
- non-skid food and water bowls
- pouch that holds treats and fastens on a belt
- stylish leash
- subscription to *Dog Fancy* magazine
- tennis balls
- travel kit that includes portable food and water bowls

Gifts to Avoid

Think safety first when selecting a gift for the canine honoree. Skip toys made of fleece with squeakers because of the risk of a puppy or dog swallowing the squeaker and choking. Same goes for any stuffed animal or toy with small, easy-to-yank-off parts like bells or felt eyes.

Keep a dog's size and personality in mind when selecting a gift. Many chew toys come in different sizes. Also, seek toys that are durable and washable.

Congratulations! By pawing through the pages of this book, you are now ready to throw a fantastic party for your favorite canine and his guests. You now have everything you need to plan, host, and do a quick after-party cleanup. You may discover dog parties bring out the party animal in you, too! Party on! Woof!